Witness

Jacob Kobina Ayiah Mensah

Contents

The House in the Hills
Periodic Chart
Dusters
Burning
Last Bridge
Winter Bodies
Street Theories
After Snow
Abandoned Position in the Late Light
Impromptu
Driving
Adding Up
At Exhibition
The Positive
Suitcase
First Summer Hour
Near Complexion
June Gloom
Edging the Limestone
Taxi Body
Tropical Storm Fay
Fence
Grunion
Illustration Water Lily
Expression Surfing
August Beings
Milky Way Avenue
Boutique Scarecrow
Persimmon
River Piss
Midday Coolness
One Hundred of Gentler Nineties
FLEDGLING
WISH

COVER GIRL

Rich colours in the wet street
and butterflies in every cover
not a smudge in sight.

All day real breakthrough news in lip
colours only from cover girl.   Clingy,

for a luscious look
and feel that really lasts,
this   cover girl

I am used to this early childhood
I am used to this early childhood

hunting in a reservoir of wild flowers
I am targeted
trapped in her definite beauty   action
looking skin every morning

in elegant opera coat
I am a lizard
trapped in Alabama

only to flop in a matter of days
on a broken glass wall—

underpriced   and forgotten
but her
long cut (over the hips)   and clean

(no epaulets or metal doodads):
peeking through semi-opaque

overlayers of the crowed street
of now flowers
with messy hair
I present my fractious mood

and she dares whisper any observations
I entreat myself
She stands soon at my knee

with a veil of gossamer on her head
I am tired

with raking swaths
and our speechless colloquy is to this effect
she owns her heaven

to change
and ring again

she pushes
unceremoniously me
to one side,   saying
I must play the accompaniment.

TOGETHER

Light out in my New York apartment   studio
I share with you at least on certain levels in the disciplines of philosophy
we colour a cosmopolitan roundelay

in oil crayons on brown wrapping papers – that combo
we all remember from elementary school
I toss   my stuff into the next   brimming composition

of the nerd purgatory of suburbia
to the neo-nerd heaven of downtown New York,
I lean back odalisque-like armchair,

waiting for voices in neither a hollow voice nor authentic proof
of existence but in my sleep,
I acquire a presence only as an old neighbour

distant resemblances are devouring from here
newspapers & summon votes sell well
the bills are seldom polite like the same echo

we hear deeply in   voices
everything of the wind is bitterly refrained in Bad & Columbus Goods
the cloud in my head is as monolithic virtue

follows the trends   & lends heavily itself to both
a black(or colour) & a white interpretation
based on the 6 pm news at the scab now descending hailstorms

Mould

I hold the darkness this time
before you so that you too can
touch the walls with bare hands.
I tear the papers into pieces
for the moulding in the starch.

You can see a faint candlelight
in the wind in a distance.
That is the memories. The steps
are closer to the ears now
from seventy-two years down.

Can you remember our guest
in this empty house? He is
the only man here in red dungarees,
you cannot reach his face.
I see the first dog he killed

before he creakedly locked
the gate. The fume from his mouth
clouds the room and it is too
late to ask questions, someone
from behind restores our tongues.

A kiss

A Maoist is reading a map
behind us in the kitchenette.
Maybe to marinate China
and tell us where we are
from grocery stores to the cafe
and name one mariachi music
in this new composition I work.
Our tongues are now maple syrup

in the marching seasons
to multicast the kibbutz;
the bigoted man has requested
again the bibliographies
for every speech we have moulded.
From this depth we must call
for plumage? Only yesterday
fifteen thousand neighbours died.

Building the world

you are bookbinder   cartographer
          historian: this body of work to be studied
and a ribbed surface to control heat release.
Your lover is a safe and natural way to keep warm
though it plays it straight, it is funny.   He will pause and change to texta.
To represent the change he will draw a paragraph and a man in relief.
To signal the pause, he will
gaze of an unquestioning moon. No other documentation will be required.

 about history. One cannot
beowulf a page with thin smears
you dont see every day. hypochondriac   phlox. the lettuce freshened in the

structured vermouth. the bullet in my   heart voided lostness loneliness.
like a

lake
          half a line of wang wei translated

          in its mind
in deepest nebbia. terminal shift
audio setting unavailable for
comment, the year turns a page -
to celebrate how ducks move and the big
noise they make! enjoining us to attend more closely
to pirate, treasure, flag and farm

Her "Lifestyle" in the magazine for sale: a painting collage for Salon des Refuses, France

girl called
Maybe to marinate China
into the rampant today of an open room. 'mojo'
and cockroaches are the hieroglyphs of home.

O observe
Features include superior one-piece moulded construction
It's not often I see you in front of me

stop traffic and families picnic
to being just a muttering

deflects reification
isn't chocolate at all-

Keep humming the latest toilet cleaner
Along the independent variable of time or narrative

Sri Lanka   29755   living
He'd idle behind,
there'll be no billy ocean

so he burned them in a bonfire at the end of the year,
I found them shrunk with the cold,
and vapour's glyphs are torn and tossed.

gathered from palaeochannels visible
The railway iron & they refused to cross, the gap of fear
   bag. the stamp isn't one youd   want or even read. cramps flower
   seems a bourgeois grandeur

pronunciation and a pun: a popular bottle of fizz (light-reading). For the part
      about
the secret drawer, so hefty
 Sight has its own methodology. Hearing too.

               and shot with liverspots like extra moons
Something with which to instrument his life on the unmasked pages of his room.

            Wrath and keyboards
half lotus
at the bar- 'is repetition still itself?'

Words once were more than writing, were their own
like a valle d'aosta autostrada
the spaces between breaths.

            Yet calling which way now Hansel

tell me
and say: Let me clean your glasses.

the novel on the cover of   the Bonnard painting. thats a clock
Coffe slurped smoke in-out
 with the Star of David
 behind him. Immediately familiar,
 steel frame mesh protective cover easy to assemble Includes adaptor 150cm tall
 touch the walls with bare hands.

BEYOND THE HEDGE

I've stepped silently, bringing a promising new treatment,
I don't even know its name, but I promise it's o.k.
paddies, it's more better living in the abandoned garden

here the owl and the bat have stayed for a decade
the greens are quiet on the pond growing more greener
bodies are radiating light & everything is wet

the street bells chime deadly & how to disappear in this wasted body,

we're going into remission
& cover everything by her health-insurance policy,
no withdrawal of your pension funds to pay for the rest, $73, 000

we decide to give it up a try in Virginia

THE MOON OF DEPRESSION

Freezing my attention for your love
New York City is still lying around on Friday night
I go back to reconstruct shadows
in shades of peacock blue
& deep terra-cotta
among the footprints
assembled before the grocer
I spray torchlight rays
over the moon peaching
high on a skyscraper above the bay
a baby's first moments of life

GETTING

Third day in the downtown
the sun is still cold

I cross the bustling shopping district

& everything is conceivable
up there in the hot office

we admire a framed crow on its target

I hide laughs on blank faces
I copy the wind's hues

back on canvasses

I remember how
two lamps were kept

in a bucket last night

to create illusion
almost as this

in front of a salesman

CITYLIGHTS

At the top of the empire building
filament lamps send the city very far in the ocean

a ship, VANITY FAIR, has arrived
bees are testing its flowers brought in from Kenya

in front of this glass pyramid i raze
with my dead hands in your soft skin like Olympia Hiawwatha line

AROUND

Back into my bony fish room after work I look around my body & anything has changed except
pages in exercise books

the skin-care crusade of the 90s is,

                              so far,

directed toward stress

        few companies that produce
fragrance-free hypoallergenic cosmetics,

                      have created the hood for the fullest, heaviest look.

I'm away from my skin colour
to reveal a shorter fringe of hair hanging on the fence

      you believe the pencil has really come into its own for the ongoing desire to look naturally

your European doctors hope this look is a medical condition of care
this bumpy business dubiously

you hold yourself up as a contouring surgery at Mount Sinai Hospital, Philadelphia
every one of us relaxes slightly & attempts

to duplicate his/her body

TIDE HIGH TIDE/ LOW TIDE

as the daughter   and sister of Pacific Ocean
going out on Sunday morning
as my part in this affair:

homework is my middle name
all vying with each other to catch
the best streets on tanning addiction

where the spring Chinook season is for gillnetting
the going is all vying with each other to catch
great strength of character   making

the right choices for lips,   cheeks and eyes
American women who rise every day
 to the challenge of breaking down the lingering gender barriers

at the borders may say grim
the Ilwaco Lighthouse on the aptly naming Patience Lost
my youthful pale glow   the sun to go down.

OBSESSION

At night, after facing the day's aggression,

I approach a large black-and-white portrait of his father's first wife
the choice is a kind of paradox
that needs to promote pale skin as attractive

saleswomen in cosmetics departments look at me admiringly, as if their products had anything to do
with my youthful pale glow.

I read her great strength of character, and her position as the first woman to lead

American dream

upfront Along with the usual greed, lust, and the other five deadly sins – it also has anorexic
wonders

– first a record store/ fashion boutique in Brixton
she lounges around her ritzy offices

we gaze at racks of clothing and shoes, cottons, silks, leather

But in the washroom she keeps phosphate-free toilet cleaner.

A picture that ran around the world
smiled in an abstracted, motherly way
she lunched on some healthy fruit

copied everywhere
I saw it in Argentina

it is where the eyes begin
in clear, blonde, brown, auburn, slate gray, and black.

She doesn't spend any of palest, palest blond
to a deep, deep, bitter brown,
and a black velvet stretch to die for
it is enough to have me like a heart-seeking missile, desperate to touch, to feel, to throw off
everything
I'm wearing and let her dress me

First Birth

The sun is rising from an old egg belonging to alchemist,

filled with aghast,
the heart of black oak is seen
beyond overgrowth.

The overdressed sky begins to overdo the garlic.

Nobody can sit in the kitchen
except the shadows of a still life in display,
the Orwellian orthotics is ossifying.

April Couple

He comes in every week
in the morning
when the sun is almost ripened orange

to break the brick wall.

He concludes

I am a stranger and she, aborigine.
His cocksure is clear and sure.

Because we have no sun to shine here.

Because she cannot write or I can see
to read my hat which is hanging

on at a cockeyed angle of the cockerel
brought in this morning to test the cog.

Complement

Your sister is the open sky.
The well-known Oddball Musing.

She has opened her doors and windows.

You handle me the chit.

The clock chimes seven.
We fly high to visit her.
But it is too hot in our midway.
Because we face the sun,
I do not know whether to continue
with you or return into my shell
far away on the earth.

No time to think or for chit-chat
we enter the smouldering clouds.
She sits in her bed waiting for me.

Completely dressed in her gypsy body,
half mohair, half moire,
she is not too bad
I used to think back at home.

She prepares two horses,
lightning and thunder,
for my cart and she joins me
for the next journey
through life loopholes.

The Sentence

My 10 years old son has just shown me
a sentence he has graffitied in a green paint:
*Your daughter was furious when she found out
you'd been reading her private letters.*

What exactly he means I do not know
except that I am midday sun, looking elsewhere,
if I can name a citizen passing by in my new world.

He is painting this world, cutting and pasting crows in the sky,

pointing to where the old post office was once sitting,
I pretend a membrane in my ear does not work,
the trail between us
becomes narrower and eventually peters out altogether.

Picker

Not partly peeping out
from behind the clouds,

not partly penciling
a penchant for fast horses

but a complete pendulum
as pimple as picturesque

on the left cheek,

I leave him alone,

standing

there in his uniform
nearly every front page today,
where the sun is shining.

Flower Wine

Soldiers who kill are cowards.
Soldiers protect the sun

with softball...

the soft-boiled sociopath looks as sodden sod
or a tablespoonful sodium bicarbonate in a glass of water.

Soft furnishings.

Check the device before you clothe your nakedness
with a folk foe's eyes in the pockets
full of rains.

Afterglow.

I wait for density
of must popular pains.

Eden

Emerging from a noun phrase
is the noontide
expanding

like that little house
grandmother has just built
inside me

is heating.

I have called my children
to come out and see
themselves again

from the beginning
in the garden of Eden,
where the eastern sun is sitting.

Affinity

Each orange in the basket
is painted in a different colour,

one is the evening sun,

but they all have the same taste
as the smouldering wood in yesterday.

But I am struggling to choose one
and walk alone to the bench in the back row.

At times
when one is returning,
I want to see with his full eyes

what is inside the palm that looks
too round and smooth than anything.

The difficult is that I do not get
the principle of affinity right
when the painting is completed.

On Display

The sounds begins
with your neighbours' laugher
at you for not able to fix
the filament lamp in your front.

The one at the top
and the other in your left rib
when you face the sun from the head.

These are the two main rain folks,

who water the farm land with hot mouth water
and cannot buy Cain ringtones.

Day by day they meet
and drink from the same broken glass.

They will shout when eating
the neighbours alive

with their hundreds of children
sitting around them and eating the droppings,

the dogs in the rehearsing scene
dart here and there taking the share.

Do not forget
the other three plus
the large family of spider web weavers
who are joint heirs.

Witness

The colours are moieties.
My eyes are moistened.

I cannot make any choice.
All the Mohican styles are plus.

They all have
the same modulus.

In this modus operandi,
I add more horse power

to cross the whirlwind,
where the whirring of the wheels

keeps us awake
all the wet sun of the midday.

Parade

The street in the jungle
has all its lights fixed.
Though it is deep night,
it is still a sunny day.

The masters hide elsewhere,
waiting to see a white lie,
whetting away.
A mane,
or leopard, or gorilla,

or any other master emerges
from nowhere to the street.

Looking at its shadow behind its whereabouts,
it howls
and turn around lazily.

The wheelbarrow wheezingly coming
drives it away.
The master goes back
to hide
and the cycle begins like the sun.

Whole

Mound beyond colours
when the sun is beyond the horizon
and the house completes itself as the centrepiece.
Manage your emotion
when the sea is steeplechase
for only two horsemen.
Manage your anger
when the body is smouldering.
Be good
when you fix
halcyon and inclement.
To enter this building of saltpetre,
where senile dementia is Semtex,
I carve semiquaver
to circumvent the distance
between carte blanche and retrenchment.
Everyone will be taxed according to his circuitry.

Calculus

Add shades. Add lights.
I do not categorise the tones.

The sun.
It is open.

No seizure.
These are voices.

Only a select few have been
invited in my painting session.

They may be Semitic.
You may be Hindustani.

He is Jew, I, an Arab.
In this painting studio,

all the workers
have themselves

as a platform to shape
self-imposed self-image.

The farmer on your left,
wearing glasses,

seldom uses brushes.
His caesarean section

is well received
by the cheerleader.

Orphan

Everything is nearby its distance in the sun.
The Catch-22, of cause, is the factor.
His mother is always checking up on him,
and he has no cheekbone to fix the checkered attire.
Painting is his child benefit. He does his tartan well.
The rest have the same heads but differences in tonnage.

Marauding

In my loincloth,
I lollipop

across the footbridge.

The marauders are far
with their sun
ahead of the Marches.

The field is fireflies.
I am blind and cannot
follow my steps after them.

Ford

First spring morning-
the street glistens
in the sweat left behind.

Passersby
hurry up.
I do not know what is happening
at the end of an arm stretched,
where the sun is in a mirror.

Everything seems the same
behind closed doors.
Maybe in its stirring.

Tom-tom Dancer

No tongue-in-cheek here.
The tart green apples

are still green and natural.

Under the green tarpaulin,
we accept nothing.

Allow her to ripen as cadence
before I take my first step.

Though your village is ahead
to treble trepidation,

I need

only your trestle in triangle.

No trial run.

We need feet.
We need the sun.

Let my busy dancer rest.

Breath

Sunshine... the butterfly
has opened its heart wide
you respond to tender act,

new life as the fresh, new course,
a motivating force. You build your abilities

in this vast grass field of the sun, in this vast human mind,
to the fullest extent possible, to where uncertainties exist and exist.

Beautiful End

Outside the fence, you look for bodies to plant in them
all the seeds gathered from the order of the memories.

Because there is no work for the planters,
weeds develop with your future,
weeds multiply rapidly between abandoned rows,
where the 92 years old cultivator tractor sits with its history.

The driver has just left with his versatile acting,
leaving the vengeful faces behind.
The unauthorised verandah becomes the venom between the ways,
that is verbatim for ventriloquist.

This verandah is collapsing
and that stream beneath will flood over there
when rains jump in suddenly,

blocking the distance between the bridges,
where I have left 50 feet behind,
behind where I can experience the sun in my dream.

Yellow Session

I walk quickly back to the kitchen. The yam on the fire is burning.
You sit in front of the television, you jump to your long legs
and in the entrance we clash. I hold you firmly and kiss
your long black hair. Because I hate destroying your taste
inside my mouth, you pull me back into the bedroom studio
when I am going away. Here you show me the new picture
of your pregnancy you have painted with the sun and hidden
on a book page. My work boots are heavy in the mud
and I cannot leave them behind, I stand in a corner looking
at things yet to be designed by us before the field is weeded
and prepared for the next years to hit us again.

Fingerprints

This is the page of paslms
of a palm `tree branches in the evening sun.

I have opened its doors and windows,
wanting to see more feet in the mud,
where I grow another world.

In bed I whisper to you
how great it is to touch
hairy spider and stick insect alive.

Construction

Under a pilgrim
autumn sun emerges
from my cloth.
Inside this wet body,
a house is swinging
on its hinges in my breath.
Someone knocks to come in for good.

Slate

I pootle to many places
to add polysyllabic steps to my slate.
Though the old carbon lamp
in my left socket is smouldering,
I have not lost the way
to where to fetch black coffee
in this bar with only one light.

No landlord Shylock.
Though there is no moon in the sky tonight
I can feel the sun and touch it. Because
a woman is busily sewing the darkness
I clothe for the public square to catch new sight.
Sitting at a table in naked
I wait to be dressed up
before the lady banker comes in
and demands the larger size of my heart.

Pomegranate

You have replanted pomegranate in place of your life.

You walk the public street everyday, hoping to achieve something.
Stocked with pills and potions of themes you are approaching,
you display your years among the still lifes

and you do not want autumn to move on.
Because it is full of the sun.

You start a journey with fresh perspectives in the sketch of an apple.

Red Wood

In the public space of a gallery,
he keeps his red wood
in the smoulderng sun.

Throughout speaking and listening, it grows.
Though visitors engage it in practical activities developed from abstract concepts,

he looses leaves after each session.

During the term-time of a day
he makes copies for himself and the rest of this little world.

The House in the Hills

There are rooms featuring your littles
like the heart and brain of a black ant.

Very difficult for visitors to climb
and come in to work with the big eyes
you paint with every colour I have come across.

You display all your examples of monographic changes
and you see your work in depth with a new response
as the sun heating this house in the September cools.

Periodic Chart

Two-tone sunny clouds.
Umpteenth time.
The rain continues unabated,
the smashed wall leans on its feet

the huge trees lie silently on the ground.

A special exhibition of sculptures. The sun in different angles.

Dusters

She sprawls on the sofa.

I scramble for the best seat in front of my mind.

A sprig of parsley is part of her mouth.
I wait on this bench in my struggling
before I go in to correct the corrections
when her sockets are reflecting from a mirror,
where I have positioned the winter sun.

I manage to complete myself, this sculpture tonight.

Burning

He refuels his energy.

His refusal to pay attention

to the turn down around the sun.

The bird under his care scoops out the seeds.
This is his registered mail
for the return flight. Regression.
The brown envelope is covered
in a large black scrawl. Misdeed.

Last Bridge

We have spent seven months here.
We cannot cross a winter raindrop in front of us.

We have borrowed ant instinct
and we need a moneylender's hand
and tomorrow sun.

This is a display of centrepiece in riddle
we ring in red with his right-handed.

The cataclysmic effects of animation
Thoreau quenched with no referee's decisions.

Winter Bodies

New York is snowing & I'm coming myself in your false arms
to see you again as big as the dark Helsinki in winter sites.
then, you'll be brightened, the 18-hour nights in my life;
then, you'll be the next snowy fescue growing on the walls
with fair skin, blue or gray eyes, & blond or light brown hair;
here I'm stuck in your body for good or bad to different language families,
still looking at myself in the eyes of the cabdrivers who don't speak English.

Street Theories

My body is sold to offer the size of your butt in the midwinter
& the street is quiet to welcome the first car that displaces its headlight
for the spirit of silence with no fits or yester-year's anger I carry about
in your new fur-trimmed tweed, a taffeta parka, suede leggings,
or the knapsack in alligator to life patterns, or see boundaries blur.
Now that you're a holy shit on the minds of New Yorkers,
let me slice your hugeness to get down to your real flesh, hiding
from the rest of my bones before I set off here to Manhattan.

After Snow

I'm the first motorbike to pollute the streets.

The smog reduce the light at dawn to trace your bony body,
& the passage to the main avenue is blocked in the sand,

I follow the tracks that lead to hell
into someone whose is an unknown cinnamon

with the branches cracking in the wet winds.

Abandoned Position in the Late Light

Whenever I touch your summit
I've something to blame myself
& you wish everything will end
According to your dictatorship.
Suddenly I'm shivering, returning
To my cold cell in the same bed.
How difficult to find your hand
Still holding your black body
Without the usual sinew & muscle
After the faith is built on the cairn.

Impromptu

I know I've promised to stop
talking about sex when we're
in bed but we're in mid-spring
& the field is green & N. Y. streets
are warm, I'm gnarled tree
in a black house, I'm sure
I've to mine my sears.
Oh just a thought to be
refined in the April rains,
no nouveau riche here.
I burn the ashes of my body smell
with your sweet fragrance
& keep the axe in its position.
Because we've introduced nuance
into the argument, how to supersede
the aristocracies of wealth & birth.
That's why I've forged my faith
into foreskin & I'm motived by
something more than the inadequacy
of breaking down class barriers.
& now that my hands, the forceps,
in your body, I'm crossing at a ford
as the forebear of forcement
& must be forearmed to know
exactly what're made of in the future.

Driving

I like being a machine, let me be
a Ford Probe LX, newly old,
for now, that makes up a body's
sleek exterior, across the U. S.
jn search of America & myself.
Am I moving away from N. Y.
to Seattle, Denver, San Francisco,
or *Philadelphia*? Here I'm poised
to expand with a deal of getting
things right, I'd try to get out
 of any body that doesn't add up
 in a tatty street surrounded by
billboards. I feel the journey
through your body to a place
I don't know & won't know.

Adding Up

Every adjective is a vegetable in our kitchen.
For example, black, or white, we wait to see
how this adds up to the aubergine soup on fire
when I keep a copy of the Zapruder film
in the VCR library in the list of busy adjectives.

At Exhibition

In the hotel lobby,
you're waiting for me

        to drop off mu duds,

we've ended up in a game on English language alphabet.

        Let *G* be words like God, gold, good, etc, you've suggested.
What about *B*? Black, body, bad,

though the lights look a bit iffy,
we're full of loony ideas in our armchairs. Get the loo out from my soul!

        When my rap cheers & shits introspectively remain data processing, I'm
waiting for another rap battle. You angrily jab a finger into my chest. We invent a better excuse than
that. & here we create careers

The Positive

The sun has sunk low on the horizon & I can see
 her lone figure standing under guava trees & from here,

let me stretch my armless body to touch the luster of her long dark hair
& at least choose who'll sway me away on this driftwood to the hotel

when I'm still locked in a pattern of a Neapolitan lady who's a wife well be
the room to be filled with light. I remain in a diplomatic talks for a new fence.

In the heart of a man, a new life begins with the story of mincing words on the lips,
& I begin my blind stitching, stitching the body I'm left with, into her care in the couch,

where I'm lying & holding the weight of her large breasts in my false hands, she likes this activity
inside her mould & woe to me when I refuse her, we gaze through our body, seeing cow carcasses

piled up in a view. We've lost our words, struggling to pick them up one after another in broken
pieces. She points to the cook who's spitting into the soup in the sumptuous room.

I've lost my appetite & for days now I've not been eating well & can't stand up.
The doctor has just left, but we've travelled far to pay our returns with goodwill.

Suitcase

Hot day & my vessel is my life, crossing the ocean with a suitcase—

I carry a suitcase, an exhibit, to the Metropolitan Museum of Art, through examples of my black body—

lives of people from thousands of miles apart are beginning to unfold in the nuclear industry—

where things are rotting to their bones, leaving only a mythical bodies behind the walls are yellow—

this suitcase isn't only unique in composition but in its range of shapes in the heat—

I'm deeply within the rusting dig, holding the remnants of hoofers—

this triangle suitcase is project of women left at home, waiting for the opportunities of war—

a photograph is burning ahead of me with its shadow of pools floating away—

I prevent her from returning to her old self after the accident & miscarriage—

in the intense blackness every noise can mean holy & what happens if the police officer I charge is losing his hearing—

the bicycle is common sense, it's complex, it's healthy & it's fun—

it'll expose its fears, fantasies, loves, thoughts, feelings & hates among the nice girls who're still hiding laugh & cry in the train—

she's a compelling body, haunting & tantalizing in the gallery—

as an unseen character is emerging from a house built on the monastery to lead players to display a warmth of despair—

I reinstate the danger, confrontation, & excitement, not ignoring the darkness falling on the side of the drink in glasses—

I declare that abstinence is the best cure for a hangover in the synthesis of language—

she stands at the sink washing up to please herself because se prefers her hair to the dog coming in—

I explore your questions in this suitcase with little breath & two diametrically opposed cultures—

First Summer Hour

This is the true hour of hotness.   I'm
 expecting you still standing

 near a body with false ears,
the idea to enter the hall
with personal progress &   the conquest of self

with a light or language
can't be reached. As we follow our heartbeat,
the only sound we can trace at this moment,

I touch with another false limbs to offer men,
who're lacking in moment of need,

this order doesn't come from you,
is only the fruit of men's fantasies

& short-lasting, they're mistaken.
By this measure I take, smelling
with false noise before I bite with al ill teeth,

I'm only hastening the decay in this wasted body now.

I'll strangle the movements of freedom

to taste my dead body in its original & permanent state,
which has been profoundly altered by modern society,

once its task is completed,
let me be protected & reformulated into oxygen.

Near Complexion

She sits at table reading
the illegible handwriting of an immigrant
who's a woman rising above
the noise of some men in the factory.

She draws her body with black Indian ink,
this busy woman with all those bounding
 children under her care we don't abide by
a system which opposes the machine counts,
she tries to tug this way for the poor voyager,
who's speeding around the sun in an orbit so dazzling, so lively,
so gay, & above all the previous civillisations in this way,
to spend time with the Cooper-Hewitt in New York.

You know she's of Syrian & Lebanese origin,
this madam who sits at the table reading
& interrupts this with drawing,
she fills her commercial-point-of-view
with Parisian fishing tackle shops, displacing flies,
hooks & floats, you watch the pool in her left eye
that lies motionless & the several free-standing stones
behind the factory emphasis her stillness.
To that direction, she looks for their contact with conscience.
This flame is alive, is in each of each, we share this discovery.

June Gloom

Packed in silence with nothing to do again,
you give me that look & I smile back.
The space is blocked in a huge body
in cloudy, overcast skies with cool temperatures,
who can stand in fear & find what's true & essential?
We don't wish to go beyond fear & project outside the individual.
The practice is a trade, his life business at the minimum of a third of his body.
If I calculate that remaining time, I'm spent as your voice
& the quantity is the profit, we repudiate progress & set
the body up against the mind, everything turns away, is crushed by the experience.

Edging the Limestone

    Finding miracles in your body,
I've encircled my senses among
the skunk cabbages & the wet field
 isn't far from the body rotting
down to it core,

                    I've come

        to be known, living
on the edge of a coral reef
in the thatched fares of Harlem streets,
it's like swimming in some
            exotic aquarium
the windows have been hurriedly
blacked out with moonlight
                coming back.

Taxi Body

So long is the silence protracted to control songs
& whispers in the gate when no hands are shaking

in confirmation of the word I carve in the cellar.
I'm sure we shan't be wasting time we've done

in your mysterious chamber, trying to fix the broken
eggs when you're quite pale with your vigils. I don't

want you to curse me for disturbing the rest of figures
I paint on the canvasses. That's why I've stopped

attending to my soul & its bitterness is causing me
to drift away from myself. Now, why're you

falsely accused of wrong-doing & shot to death?
My conscience bothers me, & I'm convince that

I've not done enough for you. This foolish flesh
I wear is rotting when someone in you is pouring

sweet oil into the dig in my heart, I replace this body

Tropical Storm Fay

A historian　　　　now is a mapper

　　　　in the flooding stories, a body

from the surface low & slowly

drifting far east end before crossing

over any panhandle & drifting across the southeastern poles

 in a new surface low, emerging off the coast of the postal coast.

The storm utilizes everything

for cyclogenesis & coalesces into itself. It intensifies before shifting west booth

& landfalling, costing deep

convection & degenerating into

a post-tropical cyclone.　　　　We waste　　　　high winds & stormy weather

with the heaviest rains, New York City Metro　　　　is flooded & impassable, my mind

is tired

　　　　to the downed trees & wires

causing power outages,

I've lost my tie. But I gaze back

 at the alignment of menhirs in the street,

the colonnade of the sea is widely opened

with household stock, your new clothes are the flyers

floating from one office to a factory, back to you as a body

Fence

This country lies in the flood

& its foundation of the fence has been shaken

& water lilies grow anytime & anywhere

& in half nakedness towards your small body

you're sinking in the wet shoeless feet in the corridor

sinking elsewhere

we're aware of this reverberations

braking into pieces

by the sound of children still ringing,

the tap of blood is running a little faster

& it seems at any moment, a body

will be fallen on this fence

& crushed away.

Grunion

I'm a sardine-sized fish

found off the California coast, I'm here spawning by laying my eggs in the sand

at high tide near midnight. I've left the crowded waves, that's now with its over-populated

confusion of bundled & squatting bodies of ocean acidification, without any physical action,

I follow a spasm of future to build a self-reproaching family.

The lights of the ship passing

by is blocking a view near future.

The presence of a plastic waste

passing by is a heavy load of the waves,

& I'm wrapped in its body. This is the mind

in a single shocking hitting the face of the rocks

covered in half a pace & half to redeem

or expiate the omission in the seabed.

Illustration Water Lily

The multiple adjectives

qualifying the American noun

echo the hopes of dead horses

abandoned in the record of a passage

largely lying between sorrow & failure

for new designing evasions

you see this, I take my leave because everything is real,

everything I say is real when I say wolves have no teeth it's real

you wonder how everything is returning to life, including all the abstract adjectives.

Expression Surfing

  Comforting a vast migration

of peoples across the continent,

across mixtures of blood,

  across ironic history of jokes,

precisely at the moment

  in time when so many

panorama pictures

are a matter of one body,

  we blame nobody

when we feel we've been made

  to stand more erect than usual,

we follow everything on stage.

I'm expected to get away

  with a photograph that's

beyond me, beyond anything.

August Beings

In an abandoned garden, full of wild aubergine

& marrow plants, & unfinished marbles lying about, I sit on a high stool

in a corner of the dilapidated ceramic workshop, carving porcelains from a hard clay. & on & on,

I look at your direction,

where you've composed

& inherited it confusion

with its more famous portraits,

I'm narrowly escaping

from its imprisonment

I bear a close resemblance

to that of a wounded cactus

this ad hoc method

of creating remains readily

available on procedure & legal questions   it's a truism to say this

Milky Way Avenue

The black pickets,

faith of victims,

reflecting the meekness they've all felt

someone discloses a message to her employee

on a new china plate

strangers listen to the winds & challenge to take the next step beyond your body

you no longer believe completely in the world here

you nonetheless, have not fully embraced your specific purposes on advisory committees

a man is the living that feigns & forges pains on the anvil,

I'm so thoroughly to manage a pain

I follow the track of our sweat & sketch a train following the visceral fat

we agree to stop calling each other names & create

new chapters on climate change & ecological emergencies

Boutique Scarecrow

I'm a fashion designer of a large firm.
The lather is my ideas
 & the ideas are all my emotions.
I think with my body
to feel how a shape is put
on a plus-sign of a pole.

To design a flower is to smell it.
To think of how to taste is to have a long tongue.

This is why she's very reluctant to ask for help
& your anger is so great against your daughter, even
the people standing around, some are in chains,
others are the convicts, your premature old age
 is the thought now. The result looks like
a gigantic dustbin, the floor is still littered
with toast crusts, you're informed that this
hospital is trying to remedy the problem
of inexperienced staff, we wait for you to hold down.

Persimmon

All over America we're burning the cooking

   & serve raw persimmon from the August farms.

   In the panty I tie your apron very quickly & its strings

   dangling loosely, announcing your presence at work.

All over America we're burning the cooking on another fire.

   We're waiting for the moment when I continue to fill unequal abilities which are
tenacious & pervasive, the admission is the paramount importance of the home

a raw deal, my pot with words of all possible meanings in the future, I help by remembering

   we're waiting to burn the cooking still babbling.

The cook with long white snow hair coughs

& spits into the big pot with soup. She clears her throat

 with a grunt, coughing & spitting into the boiling soup.

We hold our breath & go in our separate ways & meet

again in the kitchen to burn the cooking when she's away

in the main entrance. I'm the only black person in this café

& all over America we're burning the cooking.

She mutters something & goes back to the stove, coughing & spitting into a bubbling pot.

I leave where I've hidden in my body into the backyard to breathe & sip hot coffee.

Your face is pale & you ask me, "Is this true?" I hear the cook say, "Get out, nigger! I don't like your looks." I hear this thousand times a day, & while we're still unskilled among the manual workers,

all over America we're burning the cooking to serve permissions.

River Piss

Notwithstanding
the leverage,
a ridge of sediment
deposited naturally

      alongside
      anything found

you continue
& to replace lias with lobelia.
After that extensive lobotomy
words are shattered,

      fractured
      beyond

restoration. After that
massive lobotomy
family model
remains towards

      reversion
      to the median

for the upbringing of offspring
you grope your way
through the refectory,
feeling with hands

      along
      the table

you hear the sickening blow
the bones break in the body frame
in the final frantic whimpering
you seize your black skin

      in your clothing,
      pulling upright.

Midday Coolness

The peach blossom with shining leaves,

the air is wet with no water to soak us,

we visit the remains of the temple.

The apples & peaches have taken a shape,

there are several obstacles still to be removed,

the housekeeper comes out & announces

fresh complexion of leaves in the corner of the footbridge.

I imagine the faint smile on his face getting fewer & fewer,

       we follow it in the course of the conversation, where the carbon cycle.

The extinct volcano is just in a view.

You're feeling something,

something that's heavier than your body,

something that extinguishes all hope beyond the horizon,

your calm exterior hides your intense fear,

we keep at the very top of your speed until we reach the door of the small log cabin,

where the farmers have arrived some ten minutes before,

we're extolling the virtues of new life & the busy street sound isn't alterable conviction down there.

One Hundred of Gentler Nineties

In the neo-nerd heaven of downtown New York,
We join slender lovers wandering in the full moon parks.
Suddenly, we stop, embracing each other, pressing
your small body with tense fingers of steely bone
 into mine, the yellowish pink leaves in the streetlight
reveal smooth as ivory, taut under stretching flesh,
we stride forward down the central corridor
of the stringent street conditions, we're blown
from exertion, we hear voices but far away,
perhaps we've gone too far, perhaps it's all right
for a couple, a moment to sense some such relief
in the air, after she's recovered from surgical operation,
we watch the rectangle of moonlight at the far end
of the hospital, shattered in the riot, we spend
the whole night reliving our beginnings as immigrants,
I sip my hot coffee from a china mug.

FLEDGLING

turning streetlights into history long before we ever learn of them, their reflection on the floor

in Balloon House is more slippery like my language without a

throne/

I open early morning among dragonflies of elected monarchy with
heart,/ with fighting fire,/ I select your streets,/ turning them into

a newest republic

& keeping on watching footprints till I am filled with water/

as jubilant citizens of these streets

flooding over the space
to grapple with any building

I keep my end in the beginning/

& beginning from a blistering 12,700 m.p.h.
to a toe-in-the-dust touch-down speed of a few feet per second

I keep my begin in the ending/

WISH

a picture under the red metal glass glows
with your natural sight

                jettisoning its heat shield

    I keep on its puzzles
    stuffed in envelopes

on the kitchen table

      if everything in this corridor

is less obvious

      or what you have simply shrugged
      your shoulders & go away,
      I consider the American people's
      support of future offsprings

     with hopeful fatalism within
     a carrier's control, showing that

        the piece glows

Acknowledgements

"Mould", "A kiss", "Building the world" and
"Her 'Lifestyle' in the magazine for sale: a painting collage for Salon des Refuses, France" were first published by *Cordite Poetry Review*, 2009.

"OBSESSION" was first published by Adirondack Center for Writing

About the author

Jacob Kobina Ayiah Mensah[(⊤‖ |=⊔ᆨ ⊨|ᆉᆷ ᆨᅥ| ⊨⊨⊨⊔−| ℍ) (also known in the Turtle Mountains, North Dakota, as **Sitting Mountain**)], a self-made Ojibwa, Basque, Catalan, Spanish, gypsy, a Black African tribe and Greek descent and a multilingual poet, multidisciplinary artist, and algebraist, works in mixed media. His most recent poetry chapbook is *Kind Haven* (The Operating System, 2020) and a full-length poetry collection in Spanish, *agua y color*, is forthcoming from Valparaiso Poetry Press. His poetry, songs, prose, art and hybrid works have appeared in numerous journals, including *JMWW*, *Constellations*, *New Note Poetry*, *Chapter House Journal*, *Red Ogre Review*, *Newfound*, *The New Southern Fugitives*, *Inverted Syntax*, *The Elevation*, *Moon Shadow Sanctuary*, *Passenger Journal*, *Twisted Vine Literary Arts Journal*, *Millennial Pulp Literary Magazine*, among others. He lives in the southern part of Ghana, in Spain, and the Turtle Mountains, North Dakota.